HEADStart

UNDER THE SEA

First published in Great Britain by
CAXTON EDITIONS
an imprint of
The Caxton Book Company,
16 Connaught Street,
Marble Arch, London, W2 2AF.

ISBN 1 84067 057 6

A copy of the CIP data for this book is available from the British Library upon request.

With grateful thanks to Morse Modaberi who designed this book.

Created and produced for Caxton Editions by
FLAME TREE PUBLISHING,
a part of The Foundry Creative Media Company Ltd,
Crabtree Hall, Crabtree Lane,
Fulham, London, SW6 6TY.

Printed in Singapore by Star Standard Industries Pte. Ltd.

HEADstart

UNDER THE SEA

*Earth's most fascinating and
mysterious areas, explained
in glorious colour*

CAMILLA DE LA BÉDOYÈRE

CAXTON EDITIONS

~ Contents ~

Introduction

Seas and oceans are huge masses of salt water. They are where life began and underneath the rolling waves many types of animal and plant still exist. The oceans are rich in food and oxygen. They are a good home for many animals: from tiny creatures, too small to be seen with the naked eye, to the huge blue whale which is the largest animal to have ever lived on Earth, including the dinosaurs.

Oceans even control life on land; they are responsible for our weather and can give us food and energy.

Warm and cool currents of water flow through the oceans and different types of animals and plants live in these currents. The edges of the oceans are shallow, warmed by the sun and are brimming with life. The centres of the oceans are very deep, cold and dark places where creatures struggle to survive.

For centuries people have travelled the world by boat exploring new lands. Exploring under the sea has always been more difficult, however, with the use of diving equipment and craft that can carry people or robots to the ocean depths, more of the sea's secrets have been discovered over the last decades than ever before.

People can now make use of the oceans in more ways than ever in the past. With modern boats fishermen can take huge catches from the sea. Oil and gas are taken from the depths of the North Sea and the power from waves can be used to make electricity. Even old shipwrecks can be brought to shore and their ancient treasures revealed.

Seas and Oceans

When the world was created, billions of years ago, there was no water. Gases came from the hot, melting core of the Earth and these eventually became air and water.

Almost three-quarters of the Earth's surface is covered in water and most of this is the salt water of oceans and seas. There are five oceans; the Atlantic, the Pacific, the Indian, the Arctic and the Antarctic.

Oceans are huge and all of them are still growing. A long break, or trench, lies in the middle of each ocean, from which molten rock spews. This rock is added to the ridges on either side of the trench and so the ocean floor spreads.

The bottom of the ocean floor is very deep. The Marianas Trench in the Pacific Ocean is the deepest point on Earth and is 11,137 m below sea level. In comparison, Mount Everest is only 8,848 m tall!

Since the sea floor is spreading in one area it must be destroyed by the same amount elsewhere. This happens where there is a break in the Earth's crust and one part slips below another and is melted. At these places, called trenches, some of the newly melted rock escapes upwards, creating a chain of volcanoes. Sometimes these volcanoes form islands. The islands of Japan and Hawaii are volcanic.

The salt in sea water comes from rocks; rain water and rivers wash the salt out of the rocks and into the sea. All rivers flow to the sea, not away from it.

Exploring the Sea

It is natural for humans to explore the world around them and from the earliest times people have taken to boats to sail across the seas and oceans. The Polynesians began journeying 3,500 years ago and made new homes on Pacific islands. The Arabs and the Chinese were also early explorers of the oceans.

The Vikings were experienced sailors and travelled as far as North America, using the power of wind and large teams of rowers.

Some of the world's greatest explorers were Portuguese and undertook dangerous journeys to discover new lands and routes for trade.

Today, scuba divers carry tanks containing air that they can breathe through a mask. They can only stay underwater for a short while and cannot go very deep.

Some sea-craft can take people to depths of up to 3,500 metres. One of these, the *Alvin*, was used in 1985 to find the wreck of the *Titanic* and a robot called *Jason* explored the inside of the ship.

It is possible to discover what rocks lie at the bottom of the sea using deep-sea drilling. A long, hollow tube is sunk to the sea bed and samples of rock are drilled out and brought back to the surface. Ships also use sonar to map the shape of the sea bed. This is a type of sound that is passed through the water. The pattern of its echo gives information on the depth and shape of the ground far below. Most of the underwater world has been mapped this way.

Our Use of the Sea

Since humans first learned that fish could be caught we have been using the sea to get food. Not just fish, but squid, whales, seals and shellfish have been harvested from the sea.

Fishermen use different methods to catch fish. Most use nets and will throw back the creatures they do not want. Sadly, the fishermen of large fishing vessels are not so careful. Some use large suction pipes and take all the sea creatures from one place whether they want them or not. They also take all the young fish that have not yet begun breeding. This means that the vital fish stocks are becoming severely reduced and natural predators of the fish, like seals, dolphins and whales, do not have enough food.

When people first learned to make boats they did not just use them for fishing; they discovered they could travel in them. For thousands of years boats have taken explorers around the world, finding new lands and people to trade with. Our seas and oceans are still important highways that transport goods and travellers.

The movement of water can also be used to make electricity. A dam, or barrage, is built at a river's mouth and the force of the water moving through a machine creates power. This is called hydro-electricity.

We all need a small amount of salt in our diets and we also like the taste it gives to food. Salt is taken from the sea by moving sea water into large ponds and allowing the water to dry off, or evaporate, leaving the salt behind.

Ancient Sea Life

The oceans are sometimes called 'the cradle of life' because life on Earth, it is believed, began in sea water. Early life forms used water and sunlight to make food. These creatures are called cyanobacteria. They produced oxygen and this became part of the air that we breathe. Without cyanobacteria there would not be oxygen-breathing animals like us.

Over millions of years small sea creatures, with shells or skeletons made of calcium, died and fell to the sea floor. They gradually turned into rock; chalk is a rock that is made up of dead sea animals. Parts of larger animals can also sometimes be found in rock. These are called fossils and can tell us a great deal about life in the ancient oceans. It is unusual for soft-bodied animals to be turned into rock and we do not know so much about them.

From looking at fossils we know that at the time of the dinosaurs the seas were full of life. Shelled animals, called ammonites, swam through the seas like squid. Trilobites, which looked like very large woodlice, crawled along the sea floor. Ancient coral reefs grew and were home to many creatures. Some dinosaurs, ichthyosaurs and plesiosaurs, took to the sea to feed on the abundant food supply.

Sixty-five million years ago the dinosaurs died out and no one knows why. At the same time life in the sea changed greatly too; many of the ancient creatures disappeared forever, leaving only their fossilised remains.

Food of the Oceans

When microscopes were first used it was found that sea water contains many tiny creatures which were named 'plankton'.

There are a thousand different types of plankton and most of them are plants. They need sunlight to make food, so they are only found near the surface of the water where light can reach them. Plankton have no way of moving themselves and they are carried along by the wind and water currents.

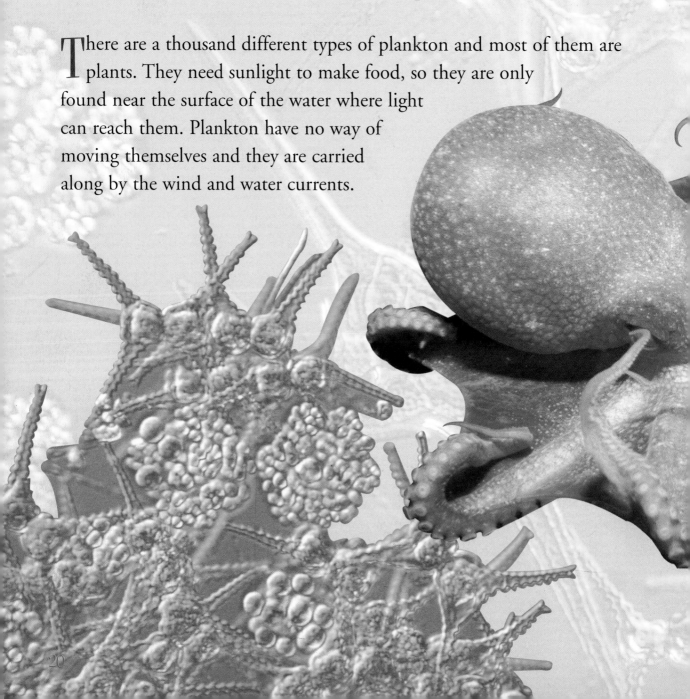

Plankton are the most important of all sea creatures because without them other plants and animals would not be able to live. Huge numbers of plankton are needed to feed the ocean animals; 200-400 billion plankton are needed every hour to feed the fish which are then eaten by one humpback whale!

Life in the oceans can be easier than in air: skeletons are not always needed because water supports the body and many animals without backbones live in the oceans. Quite often these creatures do not need to move. They can keep still and wait for food to come by, carried by the water.

Sea slugs, sponges, worms, anemones, urchins, jellyfish and octopuses are all animals without backbones. Squid and octopuses can grow to great sizes and move very quickly to escape predators.

Some sea creatures, like mussels and oysters, have shells. Lobsters and crabs have hard outer skins called exoskeletons – shells and exoskeletons protect an animal from being eaten. Like plankton, all these animals provide the food for many other creatures such as fish, seals, dolphins and whales.

The Seashore

The place where the land meets the sea is called the seashore, or coastline. Waves lap against the sand or rocks and tides go in and out. Coastlines are always changing: wind, waves, water currents and rivers flowing to the sea all change the shape of a shore.

There are two types of shore: sandy and rocky. Sandy shores are buzzing with life when the tide is high. Lugworms, sand eels, hermit crabs and shore crabs live on the sea floor but disappear when the tide is low. They dig into the sand to keep wet and to hide from any hungry seagulls. Lugworms leave tell-tale casts on the sand that look like coiled-up spaghetti.

Seaweed grows at a sandy shore but grows better at a rocky shore where it can attach itself to a rock or stone. Unlike most other plants seaweed does not take food from the ground through its roots. Instead, it takes its food from the water.

A rock pool is a good place to study the local animals as it does not usually dry out at low tide. Here, you can see beautiful sea anemones with their delicate fronds that are used for catching passing creatures. When anemones are out of water they look like lumps of jelly. Starfish wander slowly across the ground searching for food and crabs shelter behind clumps of seaweed. Shrimps dart through the water but are difficult to see because they are almost transparent. Small brown or sand-coloured fish can also be found in British rock pools.

Coral Reefs

Imagine a tiny animal, smaller than the nail on your little finger. Sitting in a cup-shaped shell this animal – called a polyp – has tentacles waving under the sea. Now try and imagine millions of polyps, squashed next to each other for kilometres, and you will be imagining part of a coral reef.

Found only in warm waters, coral reefs are huge structures made of living polyps and the hard chalky shells of dead ones. As polyps die new ones will grow on top, building the reef bigger and bigger. In fact, the Great Barrier Reef of Australia is so large that the astronauts who walked on the Moon could see it back on Earth.

Coral polyps are very fussy about where they live. The water must be clean and not too deep so that sunlight can reach them. They feed by stinging prey with their tentacles and waving the food towards their mouths. New polyps form simply by breaking a piece off an old one and then growing a new shell for protection. Not all coral looks the same; some are fan-shaped, others look like a brain.

Many types of animal and plant can live in a coral reef. The stony coral gives protection to small fish, slugs, crabs, prawns and other creatures. Divers can swim amongst the fish of the coral reefs and are often amazed by the colours and the beauty of the animals and plants around them. Reefs are fragile and divers must take great care not to damage them, as must drivers of boats skimming the water over the top of the reefs.

Fish

The first fish appeared in the seas 395 million years ago. Now there are thousands of different types of fish living from the water's edge to the deepest part of the ocean.

Fish cannot breathe air; they get oxygen by passing water through gills, which are two flaps on either side of their heads. Fish swim using their fins and strong muscles in their tails. They are usually long and smooth to make moving through water easier. Many fish swim in large groups – shoals – as this can protect them from predators.

Swordfish live alone, hunting other fish with their long snouts which gives them their name. They are fast swimmers, reaching speeds of 250 kph. They slice through shoals of fish with their 'swords' and have been known to attack boats and whales.

Some species of fish have flattened bodies so they can lie on the sea floor and hide by covering themselves with sand. Some flat fish, like rays and skates, can glide through tropical waters using flaps of skin, which are like wings. The manta ray has a 'wingspan' of 7 m. Plaice, another flatfish, can change its colour to blend in with the sea floor.

Sharks are the largest fish and are often feared by swimmers. Most sharks are harmless to people but the Great White shark does sometimes attack them, mistaking them for their normal food: dolphins and seals. Sharks are found in all the world's oceans but Great Whites are most common near California and Australia.

27

Sea Mammals I

Mammals are animals that need to breathe air. Although many mammals live in the sea they all need to come to the surface to get oxygen. Mammals also give birth to their young, rather than laying eggs, and some have to come on to land to do this.

Mammals' bodies are kept at a higher temperature than the water around them and they have thick layers of fat, or blubber, to help keep them warm.

Weddell seals live in the Antarctic, further south than any other mammal. They survive in freezing weather and can swim underwater for over an hour without breathing. Groups of seals come ashore at breeding time. The large males then fight for space and for females before mating can begin. Seals move gracefully underwater but seem clumsy when moving across land. They are hunted for their skins which people use to make fur coats – as a result some types of seal are nearly extinct.

Walruses also come on to land to mate. They live in the Arctic and use their huge tusks to pull their heavy bodies up on to the ice, as well as for fighting. Walruses also have thick whiskers which they use underwater to feel their way around.

Polar bears are good swimmers and are well adapted for life both on land and underwater. Living in the ice plains of the Arctic, polar bears are covered with a thick white coat of fur to keep them warm. Polar bears eat seals, fish, walruses and small whales. Huge claws and sharp teeth make this animal a fearsome predator of other sea mammals.

Sea Mammals II

Dolphins and whales were once believed to be giant fish because of their shape. In fact they are mammals, breathing air through blow holes on the top of their heads. They give birth to their young in the water and, unlike other sea mammals, do not ever return to land.

Dolphins live in groups known as 'schools'. They are believed to be very sociable animals and will even allow humans to join in their games. Dolphins have developed an amazing way to 'see' in the dim water using sound. They make a clicking sound that is then sent through the water; its echo returns and tells the dolphin about the size, shape and position of objects around it. This is

called echo location, or sonar, and helps the dolphin to escape predators and seek out food. Humans have developed an electronic form of sonar to enable them to search the oceans.

Some whales, like the killer whale (or orca), are meat-eaters and have teeth. They often form groups to hunt fish, seals and squid. Other whales have sieve-like plates (called 'baleen') that are used to strain tiny sea creatures called krill. Although it is the largest animal to have ever existed on earth (it is four times bigger than any known dinosaur), the blue whale survives just on krill. However, it does need to eat up to four tonnes of food a day!

Whales have been hunted for centuries because of the precious oil that is found in their bodies. Some are killed for meat and some, like sperm whales, are killed because they produce a substance called *ambergris* which is useful for making perfume. Some whalers also kill these endangered animals for sport. A few types of whale have almost become extinct and most countries have now agreed not to hunt them.

In the Deep

Sunlight cannot reach through thick layers of sea water. Once the light is gone the underwater world is dark – not the dark we are used to at night time, with light from the Moon and stars, but a total inky blackness. At a depth of 1,000 m and beyond life can still exist but because food is scarce few animals live here.

Since plants need sunlight to make food they cannot survive in the darkness of the deep. Animals, however, can feed on the food and decaying matter that drops from the sea above, or by preying on each other.

Many of these creatures are able to make their own light. This helps them to find a mate or to scare predators; some can make enough light to search for food.

The fin on the back of an angler fish is long and thin and looks a bit like a fishing rod dangling above its head. The end of the rod glows with a faint light. Unsuspecting animals mistake this light for a tasty snack and swim towards it. Too late, they realise they have swum straight into the angler fish's mouth.

Because there is very little food available in deep waters, some animals can go without food for months and will then eat whatever they catch.
Some deep sea fish can swallow prey as large as themselves.

On the very bottom of the sea floor yet more creatures live in the fine mud. Fragile animals like sea cucumbers and worms creep slowly through the ooze, grazing on sludge.

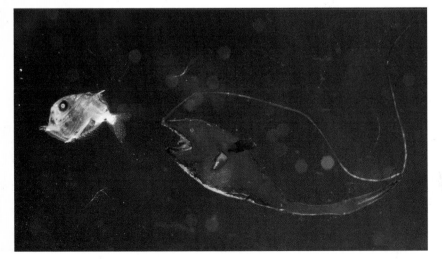

Survivors of the Sea

The sea is full of predators searching for their next meal. There are a number of good ways to try and survive; camouflage and trickery are two of these.

Many sea creatures, especially fish, use camouflage to hide themselves, either from predators or from their prey. The stonefish is well-named; lying flat on the sea floor this deadly killer looks like rocks and stones.

Some fish trick their predators with clever colouring. Stripes over a butterfly fish's eye and a pretend eye on its tail are confusing. Some butterfly fish can even swim backwards, so if are attacked they can speed off in the opposite direction. Prawns are a gritty brown colour by day but by night they become transparent and are invisible.

The hatchet fish, which lives in the ocean depths, is so thin that it is almost invisible when seen from above or below. Some types of fish are covered in mirror-like scales that reflect the light away from them. Others have stripes or broad patches of colour that help them blend into their surroundings.

Jellyfish and octopuses survive by using poison to kill their prey. This weapon is a very effective one: the venom of a box jellyfish is so powerful it can kill humans within minutes. Octopuses have eight strong tentacles for grabbing prey and a horny beak with venom for killing and eating it.

Whales and sharks have speed, strength and sharp teeth, making them d eadly killers with few natural enemies of their own.

Animal Journeys

Some animals undertake long journeys; these are called migrations. Animals migrate for different reasons; some travel to find new food, others to breed. One of the most amazing things about migrating animals is how they find their way since they do not have maps or compasses to help them.

The salmon is one of the world's greatest travellers. Pacific Salmon are born in fresh water rivers and are carried by the flowing water down to the sea. They then spend most of their lives in sea water, eating plankton at first but later eating fish.

When the salmon are adults they swim back to the American coast and manage to find the same river they were born in – it is believed that they find it by smell! Then the hardest part of the journey begins as the salmon swim upstream against the water flow. They jump up waterfalls, eventually reaching the shallow pools where they were born. The salmon mate, lay their eggs and die. The new babies now begin their long journey back to the sea.

Eels travel a great distance to breed: certain eels swim the whole way across the Atlantic Ocean. They live in rivers but when they are six years old they swim right across the ocean to the Sargasso Sea to breed. This is a journey of 6,400 km and it takes them half a year. The young eels take three years to drift back, in warm sea currents, to the rivers of Europe where the cycle can begin again.

Pollution of the Seas

Humans have been polluting the seas for many years. Oil, an important fuel, can be taken from rock under the sea. It is carried across the oceans in large ships called tankers. Unfortunately these tankers sometimes have accidents and leak toxic oil into the water.

When the *Exxon Valdiz,* a supertanker, hit rocks in Alaska in 1989 over 50 million litres of oil were spilt into the sea. 36,000 seabirds and 1,000 otters were killed and 1,600 km of coastline were affected. Some oil also sank to the bottom of the sea, forming a poisonous blanket over the plants and animals.

Fertilisers and pesticides are just two of the many chemicals that get washed in to the sea. Fertilisers cause tiny sea creatures, called plankton, to grow. This plankton may be poisonous and it also covers the surface of the sea like slime, blocking light which is needed for the sea plants to grow.

Three-quarters of the world's population lives near the coast and for centuries the sea has been seen as an easy place to get rid of rubbish of all types. Raw sewage, household waste and industrial pollutants are all dumped there.

But we are not just polluting the sea; we are also gradually heating it up. The whole planet is getting warmer because we burn fuels such as oil, gas and coal; this has serious consequences. It is now believed that if this continues the frozen waters of the ice-caps will melt and the sea-level will rise, causing towns by the coast to be flooded with sea water.

Myths of the Deep

Strong waves, sudden storms and ripping winds can whip the ocean up in minutes. Under the sea's surface life continues much as usual, but for ships and their crew a big change in the weather can spell real danger.

Long ago sailors believed that storms were caused by the sea gods. Stories and myths grew up around the sea and sailors believed it was important to keep the gods happy. The ancient Greeks believed the sea god Poseidon, brother of Zeus and Hades, was carried undersea in a chariot pulled by dolphins. They made offerings to Poseidon to keep him happy, hoping he would protect them.

To bring luck when launching a ship Romans killed a bull and Vikings slid their boats over the bodies of living prisoners. In modern times a bottle of Champagne is broken over a ship's bows when she is launched.

The myth of the mermaid is found throughout the world and they are usually believed to bring bad luck. Mermaids – half woman, half fish – are said to sing sweet songs while combing their long hair to tempt the sailors towards hidden rocks. In some stories sailors fall in love with mermaids but they always come to a watery end!

Some people have suggested that dugongs, large sea mammals also known as 'sea cows', get mistaken for mermaids but it is difficult to see how these ugly, heavy creatures could ever look like a beautiful woman.

Other stories tell of a huge sea monster, the Kraken, that can grab a ship with huge tentacles and sink it. Perhaps this myth grew after sightings of giant squid.

41

The Future

Among all the planets of the solar system only Earth has surface water. It is the special qualities of water that have made life on Earth as varied as it is. Life under the seas has changed over a long time as animals and plants have struggled to survive. From the first tiny creatures a huge range of life has developed, much of which we are only just beginning to discover.

In the future, life under the sea will undergo just as many changes as it has in the past. The oceans will still continue the cycle of growth and destruction at the trenches, changing the shape and size of both land and sea. Some types (species) of animal will become extinct and new species will replace them, just as plesiosaurs were replaced, much later, by sea mammals.

How people treat the oceans will also affect how they change. Nowadays we understand how pollution can affect animal life and some countries are trying to clean up the seas around them. If we continue to use fuels, like coal, oil and gas, we know that the world will get warmer. The ice caps will melt and the sea level will rise all around the world. This will cause flooding in many low-lying countries, like Bangladesh.

As we have learnt more about the sea we have begun to understand the importance of looking after it. If we respect the oceans now then we can continue to enjoy and explore the fascinating world under the sea in the future.

43

Further Information

Places to Visit

Anglesey Sea Zoo, Brynsiencyn, Anglesey LL61 6TQ. Telephone: 01248 430411.

Cutty Sark, Greenwich Pier, Cutty Sark Gardens, Greenwich, London SE10 9HT. Telephone (Greenwich Tourist Information) 0181 858 6376.

Deep Sea World, North Queensferry, Fife, Scotland KY11 1JR. Telephone: 01383 411880.

HMS Belfast, Morgans Lane, Tooley Street, London SE1 TJH. Telephone: 0171 407 6434.

London Aquarium, County Hall, Westminster Bridge Road, London SE1 7PB. Telephone: 0171 697 8000.

National Sea Life Centre, Brindley Place, Birmingham B1 2HL. Telephone: 0121 633 4700.

Natural History Museum, Cromwell Road, London SW7 5BD. Telephone: 0171 938 9123.

Royal Navy Submarine Museum, Haslar Jetty Riad, Gosport, Hampshire PO12 2AS. Telephone: 01705 529217.

Scottish Fisheries Museum, Harbourhead, Anstruther, Fife, Scotland KY10 3AB. Telephone: 01333 310628.

Sea Life Centre, Marine Parade, Great Yarmouth, Norfolk NR30 3AH. Telephone: 01493 330631.

Further Reading:

Whales, Dolphins and Porpoises by Mark Carwardine, Dorling Kindersley.
Seashore Animals by Michael Chinery, Kingfisher.
Planet Earth by Fiona Watt, Usborne.
The Kingfisher Book of Oceans by David Lambert, Kingfisher.
Eyewitness Guides: Shark, Shell, Seashore, Fossil, Dorling Kindersley.
Explorers by Felicity Everett & Struan Reid, Usborne.
One Small Square – Coral Reef by Donald M. Silver, McGraw-Hill.
The Sea by Nina Morgan, Kingfisher.
Sharks and Other Monsters of the Deep by Philip Steele, Dorling Kindersley.

Picture Credits

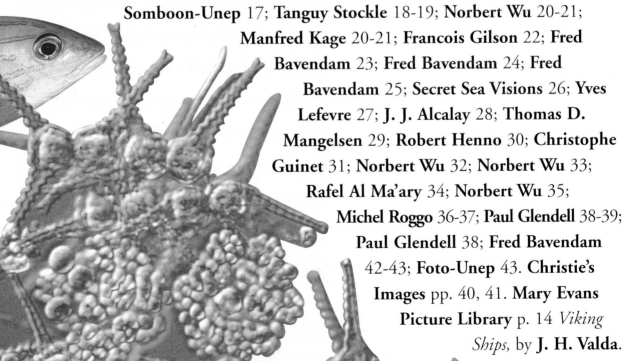

Still Pictures: pp. **Fred Bavendam** 8; **Yves Lefevre** 10; **Fred Bavendam** 11; **Juan Carlos Munoz** 12; **Alain Compost** 13; **Fred Bavendam** 15; **Thomas Raupach** 16; **Somboon-Unep** 17; **Tanguy Stockle** 18-19; **Norbert Wu** 20-21; **Manfred Kage** 20-21; **Francois Gilson** 22; **Fred Bavendam** 23; **Fred Bavendam** 24; **Fred Bavendam** 25; **Secret Sea Visions** 26; **Yves Lefevre** 27; **J. J. Alcalay** 28; **Thomas D. Mangelsen** 29; **Robert Henno** 30; **Christophe Guinet** 31; **Norbert Wu** 32; **Norbert Wu** 33; **Rafel Al Ma'ary** 34; **Norbert Wu** 35; **Michel Roggo** 36-37; **Paul Glendell** 38-39; **Paul Glendell** 38; **Fred Bavendam** 42-43; **Foto-Unep** 43. **Christie's Images** pp. 40, 41. **Mary Evans Picture Library** p. 14 *Viking Ships,* by **J. H. Valda**.